Cairn is an adventure game for one facilitator (the **Warden**) and at least one other player.

Players act as hardened adventurers exploring a dark & mysterious Wood filled with strange folk, hidden treasure, and unspeakable monstrosities.

Featuring public domain art by: Wilhelm Jordan, W. Heath Robinson, Rolf Von Hoerschelmann, Arthur Rackham, and Arthur Layard.

Written by Yochai Gal.
Text licensed under CC-BY-SA 4.0.
ISBN: 978-1-329-48902-8

I'd like to thank the following people:

Chris McDowall, for *Into The Odd*.
Ben Milton, for *Knave*.
Jim Parkin, for *Weird North*.
Gavin Norman, for *Dolmenwood*.
CosmicOrrery, for the cover design.
Tam H., for being a layout savior.
Licopeo, for the character sheet.
Lucas MacClure, for the idea.

And **Sarah**. She knows why.

For resources, hacks, and more visit:
https://cairnrpg.com

Cairn was written with the following design philosophies in mind:

Classless

A character's role or skills are not limited by a single class. Instead, the equipment they carry and their experiences defines their specialty.

Death

Characters may be powerful, but they are also vulnerable to harm in its many forms. Death is always around the corner, but it is never random or without warning.

Fiction First

Dice do not always reflect an obstacle's difficulty or its outcome. Instead, success and failure are arbitrated by the Warden in dialogue with the players, based on in-world elements.

Growth

Characters are changed through in-world advancement, gaining new skills and abilities by surviving dangerous events and overcoming obstacles.

Neutrality

The Warden's role is to portray the rules, situations, NPCs, and narrative clearly, while acting as a neutral arbiter.

Player Choice

Players should always understand the reasons behind the choices they've made and information about potential risks should be provided freely and frequently.

Principles

The Warden and the players each have guidelines that help foster a specific play experience defined by critical thinking, exploration, and an emergent narrative.

Shared Objectives

Players trust one another to engage with the shared setting, character goals, and party challenges. Therefore, the party is typically working together towards a common goal, as a team.

Principles for Wardens

Information:

Provide useful information about the game world as the characters explore it.

Players do not need to roll dice to learn about their circumstances.

Be helpful and direct with your answers to their questions.

Respond honestly, describe consistently, and always let them know they can keep asking questions.

Difficulty:

Default to context and realism rather than numbers and mechanics.

If something the players want to do is sincerely impossible, no roll will allow them to do it.

Is what the player describes and how they leverage the situation sensible? Let it happen.

Saves cover a great deal of uncertain situations and are often all that is necessary for risky actions.

Danger:

The game world produces real risk of pain and death for the player characters.

Telegraph serious danger to players when it is present. The more dangerous, the more obvious.

Put traps in plain sight and let the players take time to figure out a solution.

Give players opportunities to solve problems and interact with the world.

Choice:

Give players a solid choice to force outcomes when the situation lulls.

Use binary "so, A or B?" responses when their intentions are vague.

Work together using this conversational method to keep the game moving.

Ensure that the player character's actions leave their mark on the game world.

Preparation:

- The game world is organic, malleable and random. It intuits and makes sharp turns.
- Use random tables and generators to develop situations, not stories or plots.
- NPCs remember what the PCs say and do, and how they affect the world.
- NPCs don't want to die. Infuse their own self-interest and will to live into every personality.

Narrative Focus:

- Emergent experience of play is what matters, not math or character abilities.
- Give the players weapon trainers and personal quests to facilitate improvement and specialization.
- Pay attention to the needs and wants of the players, then put realistic opportunities in their path.
- A dagger to your throat will kill you, regardless of your expensive armor and impressive training.

Treasure:

- A Treasure is specific to the environment from where it is recovered. It tells a story.
- Treasure is highly valuable, almost always bulky, and rarely useful beyond its worth and prestige.
- Relics are not Treasure, though they are useful and interesting.
- Use **Treasure** as a lure to exotic locations under the protection of intimidating foes.

Die of Fate:

- Occasionally you will want an element of randomness (e.g. the weather, unique character knowledge, etc.).
- In these situations, roll 1d6. A roll of 4 or more generally favors the players.
- A roll of 3 or under tends to mean bad luck for the PCs or their allies.

Principles for Players

Agency:
- Attributes and related saves do not define your character. They are tools.
- Don't ask only what your character would do, ask what you would do, too.
- Be creative with your intuition, items, and connections.

Teamwork:
- Seek consensus from the other players before barreling forward.
- Stay on the same page about goals and limits, respecting each other and accomplishing more as a group than alone.

Exploration:
- Asking questions and listening to detail is more useful than any stats, items, or skills you have.
- Take the Warden's description without suspicion, but don't shy away from seeking more information.
- There is no single correct way forward.

Talking:
- Treat NPCs as if they were real people, and rely on your curiosity to safely gain information and solve problems.
- You'll find that most people are interesting and will want to talk things through before getting violent.

Caution:
- Fighting is a choice and rarely a wise one; consider whether violence is the best way to achieve your goals.
- Try to stack the odds in your favor and retreat when things seem unfavorable.

Planning:
- Think of ways to avoid your obstacles through reconnaissance, subtlety, and fact-finding.
- Do some research and ask around about your objectives.

Ambition:
- Set goals and use your meager means to take steps forward.
- Expect nothing. Earn your reputation.
- Keep things moving forward and play to see what happens.

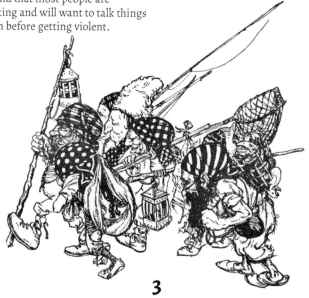

3

Character Creation

Name, Background & Traits

First, choose or roll your PC's **name** and **background** from their respective tables on page **5**. A PC's background informs their potential knowledge and skills.

Next, roll for the rest of your character's traits (appearance, speech, mannerisms, beliefs, reputation, etc.) on the **Character Traits** tables on page **6**.

Finally, roll for their **age** (2d20+10).

Ability Scores

Player Characters (PCs) have just three attributes: **Strength (STR)**, **Dexterity (DEX)**, and **Willpower (WIL)**.

When creating a PC, the player should roll d6 for each of their character's ability scores, in order. They may then swap any two of the results.

Example: Ines rolls for her character's STR, resulting in a 2, a 4 and a 6, totaling 12. The next two ability rolls result in a 9 for DEX and a 13 for WIL. She decides to swap the 12 and the 9, for a character with 9 STR, 12 DEX and 13 WIL.

Hit Protection

Roll 1d6 to determine your PC's starting **Hit Protection** (HP), which reflects their ability to avoid damage in combat.

HP does not indicate a character's health or fortitude; nor do they lose it for very long (see **Healing** on page **11**).

If an attack takes a PC's HP exactly to 0, the player must roll on the **Scars** table (page **14**).

Inventory

Characters have a total of 10 inventory slots: a *backpack* with six slots, one slot for each hand, and two slots for their upper body (such as the belt, chest, or head). The backpack can also double as an emergency sleeping bag but only if emptied of its contents.

Most items take up one slot, and small items can be bundled together. Slots are abstract and can be rearranged per the Warden's discretion.

Bulky items take up two slots and are typically two-handed or awkward to carry. Anyone carrying a full inventory (i.e. filling all 10 slots) is reduced to 0 HP.

A PC cannot carry more items than their inventory allows. Carts (which must be pulled with both hands), horses, or mules can increase inventory. **Hirelings** (page **12**) can also be paid to carry equipment.

Starting Gear

All PCs begin with:
- Three days' rations (one slot)
- A torch (one slot)
- 3d6 gold pieces

Roll once on each of the **Starting Gear** tables on page **7** to determine your PC's armor, weapons, tools, and equipment. If indicated, roll on the **Spellbooks** table on page **8** with a d100 (or roll 2d10, using one die as the ones place, and the other as the tens place). Pick only one item for each result.

See the **Equipment List** on page **9** for related armor, damage, and slot values. Smaller items can sometimes be bundled together into one slot.

If you would like something closer to traditional classes, refer to the list of **Optional Gear Packages** on page **10**.

Name & Background (d20)

Female Names

1	Agune	6	Drelil	11	Lirann	16	Sybil
2	Beatrice	7	Elgile	12	Lirathil	17	Theune
3	Breagan	8	Esme	13	Lisabeth	18	Wenlan
4	Bronwyn	9	Groua	14	Moralil	19	Ygwal
5	Cannora	10	Henaine	15	Morgwen	20	Yslen

Male Names

1	Arwel	6	Breglor	11	Grinwit	16	Melnax
2	Bevan	7	Canhoreal	12	Gruwid	17	Orthax
3	Boroth	8	Emrys	13	Gruwth	18	Triunein
4	Borrid	9	Ethex	14	Gwestin	19	Wenlan
5	Breagle	10	Gringle	15	Mannog	20	Yirmeor

Surnames

1	Abernathy	6	Crumwaller	11	Harper	16	Swinney
2	Addercap	7	Dunswallow	12	Loomer	17	Thatcher
3	Burl	8	Getri	13	Malksmilk	18	Tolmen
4	Candlewick	9	Glass	14	Smythe	19	Weaver
5	Cormick	10	Harkness	15	Sunderman	20	Wolder

Backgrounds

1	Alchemist	6	Cleric	11	Magician	16	Performer
2	Blacksmith	7	Gambler	12	Mercenary	17	Pickpocket
3	Butcher	8	Gravedigger	13	Merchant	18	Smuggler
4	Burglar	9	Herbalist	14	Miner	19	Servant
5	Carpenter	10	Hunter	15	Outlaw	20	Ranger

Character Traits (d10)

1. Physique

1	Athletic	6	Scrawny
2	Brawny	7	Short
3	Flabby	8	Statuesque
4	Lanky	9	Stout
5	Rugged	10	Towering

2. Skin

1	Birthmark	6	Round
2	Dark	7	Soft
3	Elongated	8	Tanned
4	Pockmarked	9	Tattooed
5	Rosy	10	Weathered

3. Hair

1	Bald	6	Long
2	Braided	7	Luxurious
3	Curly	8	Oily
4	Filthy	9	Wavy
5	Frizzy	10	Wispy

4. Face

1	Bony	6	Perfect
2	Broken	7	Rat-like
3	Chiseled	8	Sharp
4	Elongated	9	Square
5	Pale	10	Sunken

5. Speech

1	Blunt	6	Gravelly
2	Booming	7	Precise
3	Cryptic	8	Squeaky
4	Droning	9	Stuttering
5	Formal	10	Whispery

6. Clothing

1	Antique	6	Frayed
2	Bloody	7	Frumpy
3	Elegant	8	Livery
4	Filthy	9	Rancid
5	Foreign	10	Soiled

7. Virtue

1	Ambitious	6	Honorable
2	Cautious	7	Humble
3	Courageous	8	Merciful
4	Disciplined	9	Serene
5	Gregarious	10	Tolerant

8. Vice

1	Aggressive	6	Lazy
2	Bitter	7	Nervous
3	Craven	8	Rude
4	Deceitful	9	Vain
5	Greedy	10	Vengeful

9. Reputation

1	Ambitious	6	Loafer
2	Boor	7	Oddball
3	Dangerous	8	Repulsive
4	Entertainer	9	Respected
5	Honest	10	Wise

10. Misfortunes

1	Abandoned	6	Defrauded
2	Addicted	7	Demoted
3	Blackmailed	8	Discredited
4	Condemned	9	Disowned
5	Cursed	10	Exiled

Starting Gear (d20)

Armor

1-3	4-14	15-19	20
None	Brigandine	Chainmail	Plate

Helmets and Shields

1-13	14-16	17-19	20
None	Helmet	Shield	Helmet & Shield

Weapons

1-5	6-14	15-19	20
Dagger, Cudgel, Staff	Sword, Mace, Axe	Longbow, Crossbow, Sling	Halberd, War Hammer, Battleaxe

Expeditionary Gear

1	Air Bladder	6	Fire Oil	11	Manacles	16	Rope (25f
2	Antitoxin	7	Grappling Hook	12	Pick	17	Spirit Wa
3	Cart (+4 slots, bulky)	8	Large Sack	13	Pole (10ft)	18	Spyglass
4	Chain (10ft)	9	Large Trap	14	Pulley	19	Tinderbo
5	Dowsing Rod	10	Lockpicks	15	Repellent	20	Wolfsbar

Tools

1	Bellows	6	Cook Pots	11	Grease	16	Net
2	Bucket	7	Crowbar	12	Hammer	17	Saw
3	Caltrops	8	Drill	13	Hourglass	18	Sealant
4	Chalk	9	Fishing Rod	14	Metal File	19	Shovel
5	Chisel	10	Glue	15	Nails	20	Tongs

Trinkets

1	Bottle	6	Horn	11	Mirror	16	Soap
2	Card Deck	7	Incense	12	Perfume	17	Sponge
3	Dice Set	8	Instrument	13	Quill & Ink	18	Tar Pot
4	Face Paint	9	Lens	14	Salt Pack	19	Twine
5	Fake Jewels	10	Marbles	15	Small Bell	20	Whistle

Bonus Item (roll on table indicated)

1-5	6-13	14-17	18-20
Tool or Trinket	Expeditionary Gear	Armor or Weapon	Spellbook (page 8)

Spellbooks (d100)

Spell Descriptions: Pages 16-18

Adhere	26. Earthquake	51. Masquerade	76. Smoke Form
Anchor	27. Elasticity	52. Miniaturize	77. Sniff
Animate Object	28. Elemental Wall	53. Mirror Image	78. Snuff
Anthropomorphize	29. Filch	54. Mirrorwalk	79. Sort
Arcane Eye	30. Flare	55. Multiarm	80. Spectacle
Astral Prison	31. Fog Cloud	56. Night Sphere	81. Spellsaw
Attract	32. Frenzy	57. Objectify	82. Spider Climb
Auditory Illusion	33. Gate	58. Ooze Form	83. Summon Cube
Babble	34. Gravity Shift	59. Pacify	84. Swarm
Bait Flower	35. Greed	60. Phobia	85. Telekinesis
Beast Form	36. Haste	61. Pit	86. Telepathy
Befuddle	37. Hatred	62. Primal Surge	87. Teleport
Body Swap	38. Hear Whispers	63. Push/Pull	88. Target Lure
Charm	39. Hover	64. Raise Dead	89. Thicket
Command	40. Hypnotize	65. Raise Spirit	90. Summon Idol
Comprehend	41. Icy Touch	66. Read Mind	91. Time Control
Cone of Foam	42. Identify Owner	67. Repel	92. True Sight
Control Plants	43. Illuminate	68. Scry	93. Upwell
Control Weather	44. Invisible Tether	69. Sculpt Elements	94. Vision
Cure Wounds	45. Knock	70. Sense	95. Visual Illusion
Deafen	46. Leap	71. Shield	96. Ward
Detect Magic	47. Liquid Air	72. Shroud	97. Web
Disassemble	48. Magic Dampener	73. Shuffle	98. Widget
Disguise	49. Manse	74. Sleep	99. Wizard Mark
Displace	50. Marble Craze	75. Slick	100. X-Ray Vision

Equipment List (Prices in Gold Pieces)

Armor

Shield (+1 Armor)	1
Helmet (+1 Armor)	1
Gambeson (+1 Armor)	1
Brigandine (1 Armor, bulky)	2
Chainmail (2 Armor, bulky)	4
Plate (3 Armor, bulky)	6

Weapons

Dagger, Cudgel, Sickle, Staff, etc. (d6 damage)	
Spear, Sword, Mace, Axe, Flail, etc. (d8 damage)	1
Halberd, War Hammer, Long Sword, etc. (d10 damage, bulky)	2
Sling (d4 damage)	
Bow (d6 damage, bulky)	2
Crossbow (d8 damage, bulky)	3

Gear & Tools

Air Bladder	5	Large Trap	2
Bellows	10	Large Sponge	
Bedroll	5	Lens	1
Book	50	Lockpicks	2
Bucket	5	Manacles	1
Caltrops	10	Metal File	
Cart (+4 slots, bulky)	30	Mirror	
Chain (10ft)	10	Mule (+6 slots, slow)	3
Chalk	1	Net	1
Chisel	5	Oilskin Bag	
Cook Pots	10	Pick	1
Crowbar	10	Pulley	1
Drill (Manual)	10	Pole (10ft)	
Face Paint	10	Quill & Ink	1
Fire Oil	10	Rations (three days' worth)	1
Fishing Rod	10	Rope (25ft)	
Glass Marbles	5	Saw	
Glue	5	Sack	
Grease	10	Shovel	
Grappling Hook	25	Soap	
Hammer	5	Spike	
Holy Water	25	Spiked Boots	
Horn	10	Spyglass	4
Horse (+4 slots)	75	Tar	1
Hourglass	50	Tent (fits 2 people, bulky)	2
Incense	10	Torch	
Ladder (bulky, 10ft)	10	Wagon (+8 slots, slow)	20
Lantern & Oil	10	Wolfsbane	1

Optional Gear Packages

Cleric
War Hammer (d10, bulky)
Chainmail (2 Armor, bulky)
Gauntlets (+1 Armor)
Cleansing Blade (d6)
Holy Symbol (*Ward* once per day)
Cloak of the Order

Dowser
Sickle (d6)
Patchwork doublet (+1 Armor)
Dowsing Rod
Dyestone (*Sense* if placed in fresh water)
Worn Map
Spyglass

Dwarf
Prickly Root (d6)
Pinecone Lattice (1 Armor)
Trowel
Jar of Forest Ants
Poisonous mushroom
Hand Drill

Elf
Elegant Sword (d8)
Recurve Bow (d8)
Gilt Clothing (1 Armor)
Spellbook (*Charm* or *Detect Magic*)
Golden Flute
Air Bladder

Fighter
Glaive (d10, bulky)
Scimitar (d8)
Shortsword (d6)
Shortsword (d6)
Tobacco Pouch & Pipe
Dice Set

Friar
Scepter (d6)
Deceptive Robes (+1 Armor)
Censer & Holy Water
Jug of Honey Wine
Folk Songbook
Cart (+4 slots, bulky)

Knight
Long sword (d10, bulky)
Chainmail (2 Armor, bulky)
Helmet (+1 Armor)
Heraldic Cape
Manacles
Fine Rope

Magic User
Fizzled Staff (d8, bulky)
Dagger (d6)
Spellbook (random spell)
Spellbook (random spell)
Ragged clothing (hidden pockets)
Leycap (x2, see **Relics**)

Ranger
Longbow (d8, bulky)
Hatchet (d6)
Padded Leathers (1 Armor)
Large Trap
Bloodhound | 2 HP, 12 DEX, bite (d6)
Thundering Horn

Thief
Two daggers (d6+d6)
Hooded Jerkin (1 Armor)
Lockpicks
Caltrops
Grappling Hook
Metal File

Rules

Abilities

Each of the three **abilities** are used in different circumstances (see **saves**, below).

Strength (STR): Used for saves requiring physical power, like lifting gates, bending bars, resisting poison, etc.

Dexterity (DEX): Used for saves requiring poise, speed, and reflexes like dodging, climbing, sneaking, balancing, etc.

Willpower (WIL): Used for saves to persuade, deceive, interrogate, intimidate, charm, provoke, manipulate spells, etc.

Saves

A save is a roll to avoid bad outcomes from risky choices and circumstances. PCs roll a d20 for an appropriate ability score. If they roll *equal to or under that ability score*, they pass. Otherwise, they fail. A 1 is always a success, and a 20 is always a failure.

Example: *Bea encounters a group of heavily-armed Goblins standing guard before a tunnel entrance. Her player carefully plots a course, recognizing that her 13 DEX makes sneaking past the guards the best option. She rolls a d20, and resulting in a 10 – a success!*

Healing

Resting for a few moments and having a drink of water restores lost HP but leaves the party exposed. Ability loss (see page **14**) can usually be restored with a week's rest facilitated by a healer or other appropriate source of expertise. Some of these services are free, while magical or more expedient means of recovery may come at a cost.

Deprivation & Fatigue

A PC **deprived** of a crucial need (such as food or rest) is unable to recover HP or ability scores.

Anyone deprived for more than a day adds **Fatigue** to their inventory, one for each day. Each Fatigue occupies one slot and lasts until the PC can recuperate safely for a full night, after which they recover *all* occupied slots.

PCs can also gain Fatigue by **casting spells** or through events in the fiction.

Armor

Before calculating damage to HP, subtract the target's **Armor** value from the result of damage rolls. Shields and similar armor provides a bonus defense (e.g. +1 Armor), but only while the item is held or worn. No one can have more than 3 Armor.

Shields, gauntlets, and helms may provide additional benefits according to their use.

NPCs

Reactions
When the PCs encounter an NPC whose reaction to the party is not obvious, the Warden may roll 2d6 and consult the following table:

2	3-5	6-8	9-11	12
Hostile	Wary	Curious	Kind	Helpful

Morale
Enemies must pass a WIL save to avoid fleeing when they take their first casualty and again when they lose half their number.

Some groups may use their *leader's* WIL in place of their own. Lone foes must save when they're reduced to 0 HP. Morale does not affect PCs.

11

Wealth & Treasure

The most common coin is the gold piece (gp), which is equal to 10 silver pieces (sp) and 100 copper pieces (cp).

Treasure is highly valuable, usually bulky, and rarely useful beyond its value. It can be a lure, taking PCs to exotic and even dangerous locations, and is often under the protection of intimidating foes.

Villages, strongholds, and ports of call barter and trade based on the local rarity and value of an item or commodity.

Hirelings

PCs can hire **hirelings** to aid them in their expeditions. To create a hireling, roll 3d6 for each ability score, then give them 1d6 HP and a simple weapon (d6), then roll on the **Character Creation** tables to further flesh them out. Hirelings cost between 1-3gp per day, or a share of whatever treasure the party obtains.

Spellbooks & Scrolls

Spellbooks contain a single spell and take up one slot. They cannot be transcribed or created; instead they are recovered from places like tombs, dungeons, and manors.

Spellbooks sometimes display unusual properties or limitations, such as producing a foul or unearthly smell when opened, possessing an innate intelligence, or being legible only when held in moonlight.

Spellbooks will attract the attention of those who seek the arcane power within, and it is considered dangerous to display them openly.

Scrolls are similar to Spellbooks, however:
- They do not take up an inventory slot.
- They do not cause fatigue.
- They disappear after one use.

Casting Spells

Anyone can cast a spell by holding a Spellbook in *both hands* and reading its contents aloud. They must then add a Fatigue to inventory, occupying one slot.

Given time and safety, PCs can *enhance* a spell's impact (e.g., affecting multiple targets, increasing its power, etc.) without any additional cost.

If the PC is *deprived* or in danger, the Warden may require a PC to make a WIL save to avoid any ill-effects from casting the spell. Consequences of failure are on par with the intended effect, and may result in added Fatigue, the destruction of the Spellbook, injury, and even death.

Relics

Relics are items imbued with a magical spell or power. They do not cause Fatigue. Relics usually have a limited use, as well as a recharge condition. A few examples:

Honeyclasp, 3 charges. A rusted ring that shrinks the bearer to 6"tall. Recharge: place in a thimble-sized cup of royal jelly.

Falconer's Friend, 1 charge. A bolt-shaped wand carrying the *Haste* spell. Recharge: fire from a crossbow and recover.

Staff of Silence, 1 charge. This blackened rod temporarily disables all magic within 50ft. Recharge: bathe in the light of a full moon.

Leycap, 1 use. Anyone ingesting this green-flecked mushroom loses a Fatigue, but is then required to make a WIL save to avoid its addictive properties. A fail leaves the PC *deprived* and unable to focus until they can eat another leycap, providing only a brief reprieve from the addiction.

Combat

Rounds

The game typically plays without strict time accounting. In a fight or circumstance where timing is helpful, use rounds to keep track of when something occurs. A **round** is roughly ten seconds of in-game time and is comprised of turns.

Actions

On their turn, a character may move up to 40ft and take up to one action. This may be *casting a spell*, *attacking*, making a second *move*, or some other reasonable action.

Each round, the PCs declare what they are doing before dice are rolled. If a character attempts something risky, the Warden calls for a save for appropriate players or NPCs.

Turns

The Warden will telegraph the most likely actions taken by NPCs or monsters. At the start of combat, each PC must make a DEX save to act before their opponents.

Example: Bea has accidentally stumbled onto the stomping grounds of a massive Wood Troll. In order to make a move before the Troll, she makes a DEX save. She fails, and the Troll gets to attack first.

Attacking & Damage

The attacker rolls their weapon die and subtracts the target's armor, then deals the remaining total to their opponent's HP. Unarmed attacks always do 1d4 damage.

Example: The Wood Troll roars, swinging its club at Bea, who has 5 HP. The club does 1d10 damage and the Warden rolls a 4. They subtract 1 to account for Bea's leather armor, leaving Bea with 2 HP remaining.

Multiple Attackers

If multiple attackers target the same foe, roll all damage dice and keep the single highest result.

Attack Modifiers

If fighting from a position of weakness (such as through cover or with bound hands), the attack is **impaired** and the attacker must roll 1d4 damage *regardless* of the damage die used during the attack.

If fighting from a position of advantage (such as against a helpless foe or through a daring maneuver), the attack is **enhanced**, allowing the attacker to roll 1d12 damage instead of their normal die.

Dual Weapons

If attacking with two weapons at the same time, roll both damage dice and keep the single highest result.

Blast

Attacks with the **blast** quality affect all targets in the noted area, rolling separately for each affected character. Blast refers to anything from explosions to huge cleaving onslaughts to the impact of a meteorite. If unsure how many targets can be affected, roll the related damage die for a result.

Critical Damage

Damage that reduces a target's HP below zero decreases a target's STR by the amount remaining. They must then make a STR save to avoid **critical damage**. Additionally, enemies will have special abilities or effects that are triggered when their target fails a critical damage save.

Any PC that suffers critical damage cannot do anything but crawl weakly, grasping at life. If given aid and rest, they will stabilize. If left untreated, they die within the hour.

Scars

When damage to a PC reduces their HP to exactly 0, they are sometimes changed irrevocably. See the **Scars** table on the following page for more.

C's STR is reduced to 0, they die.
ir DEX is reduced to 0, they are
yzed. If their WIL is reduced to 0,
are delirious.

olete DEX and WIL loss renders the
cter unable to act until they are
red through extended rest or by
ordinary means.

nsciousness & Death

n a character dies, the player is free
eate a new character or take control
hireling. They immediately join the
in order to reduce downtime.

Detachments

Large groups of similar combatants fighting together are treated as a single **detachment**. When a detachment takes critical damage, it is routed or significantly weakened. When it reaches 0 STR, it is destroyed.

Attacks against detachments by individuals are impaired (excluding blast damage). Attacks against individuals by detachments are enhanced and deal blast damage.

Retreat

Running away from a dire situation always requires a successful DEX save, as well as a safe destination to run to.

rs

n an attack reduces a PC's HP to exactly 0, they are uniquely impacted.
up the result on the table below based on the *total* damage taken:

asting Scar: Roll 1d6 | 1: Neck, 2: Hands, 3: Eye, 4: Chest, 5: Legs, 6: Ear.
oll 1d6. If the total is higher than your max HP, take the new result.

attling Blow: You're disoriented and shaken. Describe how you refocus.
oll 1d6. If the total is higher than your max HP, take the new result.

Walloped: You're sent flying and land flat on your face, winded. You are deprived
ntil you rest for a few hours. Then, roll 1d6. Add that amount to your max HP.

Broken Limb: Roll 1d6 | 1-2: Leg, 3-4: Arm, 5: Rib, 6: Skull.
nce mended, roll 2d6. If the total is higher than your max HP, take the new result.

Diseased: You're afflicted with a gross, uncomfortable infection. When you get over
, roll 2d6. If the total is higher than your max HP, take the new result.

Reorienting Head Wound: Roll 1d6 | 1-2: STR, 3-4: DEX, 5-6: WIL.
oll 3d6. If the total is higher than your current ability score, take the new result.

Hamstrung: You can barely move until you get serious help and rest. After
ecovery, roll 3d6. If the total is higher than your max DEX, take the new result.

Deafened: You cannot hear anything until you find extraordinary aid. Regardless,
nake a WIL save. If you pass, increase your max WIL by 1d4.

e-brained: Some hidden part of your psyche is knocked loose.
oll 3d6. If the total is higher than your max WIL, take the new result.

undered: An appendage is torn off, crippled or useless. The Warden will tell you
hich. Then, make a WIL save. If you pass, increase your max WIL by 1d6.

Mortal Wound: You are *deprived* and out of action. You die in one hour unless
ealed. Upon recovery, roll 2d6. Take the new result as your max HP.

Doomed: Death seemed ever so close, but somehow you survived. If your next save
gainst critical damage is a fail, you die horribly. If you pass, roll 3d6. If the total is
igher than your max HP, take the new result.

Bestiary

Root Goblin
4 HP, 8 STR, 14 DEX, 8 WIL, spear (d6)

- Avoid combat unless they have the advantage (such as greater numbers).
- Guard their stolen goods to the death.
- Prize Spellbooks; willing to trade.

Hooded Men
12 HP, 9 STR, 12 DEX, 14 WIL, leystaff (d8), a Spellbook (Choose one: *Charm, Hypnotize, Push/Pull, Shield*)

- The Watchers of the Wood; a cult that derive their power from leylines, rune stones, and the like.
- Critical damage: leech a part of the victim's soul (1d4 WIL damage).

Cobblehounds
12 HP, 2 Armor, 14 STR, 1 DEX, 8 WIL, bite (d10)

- Immobile constructs typically used as guardians to great tombs or artifacts.
- Unaffected by mundane persuasion techniques - but do love a good bone.

Wood Troll
12 HP, 15 STR, 12 DEX, 7 WIL, claws and bite (d8+d8 blast)

- As an action, can recover lost HP.
- Critical damage: moss and twigs begin growing out of target's wounds.

Frost Elf
14 HP, 1 Armor, 8 STR, 13 DEX, 14 WIL, icicle dagger (d6), a Spellbook (Choose one: *Sleep, Teleport, Detect Magic*)

- Beautiful, amoral, and long-lived.
- Resistant to most forms of magic.

Boggart
3 HP, 4 STR, 17 DEX, 13 WIL

- A wild, hairy trickster that takes pleasure in being a minor nuisance.
- Prizes relics and shiny trinkets above all else but unwilling to trade for coin.
- Boggarts have names that describe their true nature. Knowing their true name allows one to control a Boggart.

Creating Monsters

Use the following template to model any more sophisticated Monster or NPC:

Name
X HP, X Armor, X STR, X DEX, X WIL, Weapon (dX, special items, qualities)

- Engaging descriptor of appearance or demeanor
- Quirk, tactic, or peculiarity making th. NPC unique
- Special effect or critical damage consequence

General Principles
Ability Scores: 3 is deficient, 6 is weak, 10 is average, 14 is noteworthy, and 18 is legendary. Adjust as necessary.

Give average creatures 3 HP, give hardy ones 6 HP, and serious threats get 10+ H.

Use flavor and style to help them stand out. Players will remember a pig-faced humanoid looking for his missing sheep more easily than a generic goblin archer.

Use critical damage to lean into the thre. or strangeness of any aggressive NPC.

Remember that HP is **Hit Protection**, not *Hit Points*. It's a measure of resilience, luck, and gumption - not health.

Converting from OSR Games
- Give 1 HP per HD for most creatures.
- Most humanoids have at least 4 HP.
- **Morale** can also be used as a baseline.

Some pointers:
- Is it good at avoiding a hit? Give it HP.
- Does it soak up damage? Give it Armo
- Is it strong? Give it a high STR.
- Is it nimble? Give it high DEX.
- Is it charismatic? Give it high WIL.

Damage die are roughly the same, thoug armed attacks do at least 1d6 damage.

1. **Adhere:** An object is covered in extremely sticky slime.

2. **Anchor:** A strong wire sprouts from your arms, affixing itself to two points within 50ft on each side.

3. **Animate Object:** An object obeys your commands as best it can.

4. **Anthropomorphize:** An animal either gains human intelligence or human appearance for one day.

5. **Arcane Eye:** You can see through a magical floating eyeball that flies around at your command.

6. **Astral Prison:** An object is frozen in time and space within an invulnerable crystal shell.

7. **Attract:** Two objects are strongly magnetically attracted to each other if they come within 10 feet.

8. **Auditory Illusion:** You create illusory sounds that seem to come from a direction of your choice.

9. **Babble:** A creature must loudly and clearly repeat everything you think. It is otherwise mute.

10. **Bait Flower:** A plant sprouts from the ground that emanates the smell of decaying flesh.

11. **Beast Form:** You and your possessions transform into a mundane animal.

12. **Befuddle:** A creature of your choice is unable to form new short-term memories for the duration of the spell.

13. **Body Swap:** You switch bodies with a creature you touch. If one body dies, the other dies as well.

14. **Charm:** A creature you can see treats you as a friend.

15. **Comprehend:** You become fluent in all languages for a short while.

16. **Command:** A target obeys a single three-word command that does not cause it harm.

17. **Cone of Foam:** Dense foam sprays from your hand, coating the target.

18. **Control Plants:** Nearby plants and trees obey you and gain the ability to move at a slow pace.

19. **Control Weather:** You may alter the type of weather at will, but you do not otherwise control it.

20. **Cure Wounds:** Restore 1d4 STR per day to a creature you can touch.

21. **Deafen:** All nearby creatures are deafened.

22. **Detect Magic:** You can see or hear nearby magical auras.

23. **Disassemble:** Any of your body parts may be detached and reattached at will, without causing pain or damage. You can still control them.

24. **Disguise:** You may alter the appearance of one character at will as long as they remain humanoid. Attempts to duplicate other characters will seem uncanny.

25. **Displace:** An object appears to be up to 15ft from its actual position.

26. **Earthquake:** The ground begins shaking violently. Structures may be damaged or collapse.

27. **Elasticity:** Your body can stretch up to 10ft.

28. **Elemental Wall:** A straight wall of ice or fire 50ft long and 10ft high rises from the ground.

29. **Filch:** A visible item teleports to your hands.

30. **Flare:** A bright ball of energy fires a trail of light into the sky, revealing your location to friend or foe.

31. **Fog Cloud:** A dense fog spreads out from you.

32. **Frenzy:** A nearby creature erupts in a frenzy of violence.

33. **Gate:** A portal to a random plane opens.

34. Gravity Shift: You can change the direction of gravity, but only for yourself.

35. Greed: A creature develops the overwhelming urge to possess a visible item of your choice.

36. Haste: Your movement speed is tripled.

37. Hatred: A creature develops a deep hatred of another creature or group and wishes to destroy them.

38. Hear Whispers: You can hear faint sounds clearly.

39. Hover: An object hovers, frictionless, 2ft above the ground. It can hold up to one humanoid.

40. Hypnotize: A creature enters a trance and will truthfully answer one yes or no question you ask it.

41. Icy Touch: A thick ice layer spreads across a touched surface, up to 10ft in radius.

42. Identify Owner: Letters appear over the object you touch, spelling out the name of the object's owners, if there are any.

43. Illuminate: A floating light moves as you command.

44. Invisible Tether: Two objects within 10ft of each other cannot be moved more than 10ft apart.

45. Knock: A nearby mundane or magical lock unlocks – loudly.

46. Leap: You jump up to 10ft high, once.

47. Liquid Air: The air around you becomes swimmable.

48. Magic Dampener: All nearby magical effects have their effectiveness halved.

49. Manse: A sturdy, furnished cottage appears for 12 hours. You can permit and forbid entry to it at will.

50. Marble Craze: Your pockets are full of marbles, and will refill every 30 seconds.

51. Masquerade: A character's appearance and voice becomes identical to those of a character you touch.

52. Miniaturize: A creature you touch is shrunk down to the size of a mouse.

53. Mirror Image: An illusory duplicate of yourself appears and is under your control.

54. Mirrorwalk: A mirror becomes a gateway to another mirror that you looked into today.

55. Multiarm: You temporarily gain an extra arm.

56. Night Sphere: A 50ft wide sphere of darkness displaying the night sky appears before you.

57. Objectify: You become any inanimate object between the size of a grand piano and an apple.

58. Ooze Form: You become a living jelly.

59. Pacify: A creature near you has an aversion to violence.

60. Phobia: A nearby creature becomes terrified of an object of your choice.

61. Pit: A pit 10ft wide and 10ft deep opens in the ground.

62. Primal Surge: A creature rapidly evolves into a future version of its species.

63. Push/Pull: An object of any size is pulled directly towards you or pushed directly away from you with the strength of one man.

64. Raise Dead: A skeleton rises from the ground to serve you. They are incredibly stupid and can only obey simple orders.

65. Raise Spirit: The spirit of a nearby corpse manifests and will answer 1 question.

66. Read Mind: You can hear the surface thoughts of nearby creatures.

67. Repel: Two objects are strongly magnetically repelled from each other within 10 feet.

68. Scry: You can see through the eyes of a creature you touched earlier today.

69. Sculpt Elements: Inanimate material behaves like clay in your hands.

70. Sense: Choose one kind of object (key, gold, arrow, jug, etc.). You can sense the nearest example.

71. Shield: A creature you touch is protected from mundane attacks for one minute.

72. Shroud: A creature you touch is invisible until they move.

73. Shuffle: Two creatures you can see instantly switch places.

74. Sleep: A creature you can see falls into a light sleep.

75. Slick: Every surface in a 30ft radius becomes extremely slippery.

76. Smoke Form: Your body becomes a living smoke that you can control.

77. Sniff: You can smell even the faintest traces of scents.

78. Snuff: The source of any mundane light you can see is instantly snuffed out.

79. Sort: Inanimate items sort themselves according to categories you set.

80. Spectacle: A clearly false but impressive illusion of your choice appears, under your control. It may be up to the size of a palace and has full motion and sound.

81. Spellsaw: A whirling blade flies from your chest, clearing any plant material in its way. It is otherwise harmless.

82. Spider Climb: You can climb surfaces like a spider.

83. Summon Cube: Once per second you may summon or banish a 3-foot-wide cube of earth. New cubes must be affixed to the earth or to other cubes.

84. Swarm: You become a swarm of crows, rats, or piranhas. You can only be harmed by blast attacks.

85. Telekinesis: You may mentally move 1 item under 60lbs.

86. Telepathy: Two creatures can hear each other's thoughts, no matter how far apart.

87. Teleport: An object or person you can see is transported from one place to another in a 50ft radius.

88. Target Lure: An object you touch becomes the target of any nearby spell.

89. Thicket: A thicket of trees and dense brush up to 50ft wide suddenly sprouts up.

90. Summon Idol: A carved stone statue the size of a mule rises from the ground.

91. Time Control: Time in a 50ft bubble slows down or increases by 10% for 30 seconds.

92. True Sight: You see through all nearby illusions.

93. Upwell: A spring of seawater appears.

94. Vision: You completely control what a creature sees.

95. Visual Illusion: A silent, immobile, room-sized illusion of your choice appears.

96. Ward: A silver circle 50ft across appears on the ground. Choose one species that cannot cross it.

97. Web: Your wrists shoot thick webbing.

98. Widget: A primitive version of a drawn tool or item appears before you and disappears after a short time.

99. Wizard Mark: Your finger can shoot a stream of ulfire-colored paint. This paint is only visible to you and can be seen at any distance, even through solid objects

100. X-Ray Vision: You can see through walls, dirt, clothing, etc.

CAIRN

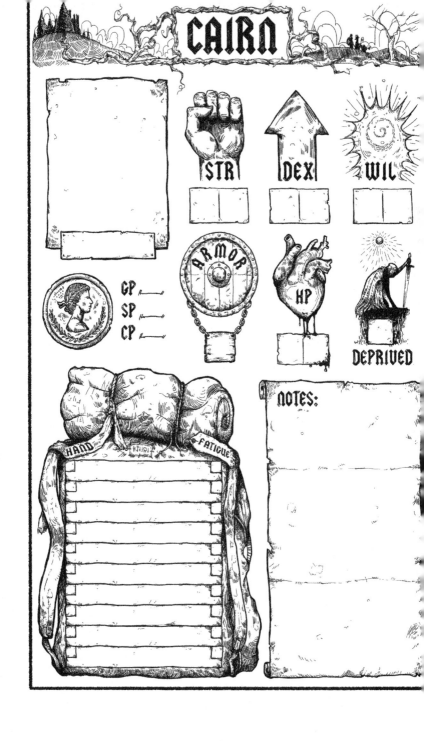

STR

DEX

WIL

ARMOR

HP

DEPRIVED

GP
SP
CP

HAND   FATIGUE

NOTES:

ABILITIES

'R: Brawn, prowess & resistance.

:X: Dodging, sneaking & reflexes.

IL: Persuasion, intimidation & magic.

SAVES

ll a d20 equal to or under an ability.
always a success, 20 is always a failure.

HIT PROTECTION

' indicates a PC's ability to avoid getting
rt. It is lost during combat & recovered
er a few moment's rest.

INVENTORY

s have 10 inventory slots: four on their
ly and six in their backpack (which acts
a sleeping bag if emptied). Most items
:e up one slot, but smaller items can be
ndled. **Bulky** items take up two slots
d are awkward or difficult to carry.
ing all ten item slots reduces a PC to 0
?. PCs cannot carry more than their
entory allows, though carts & horses
y provide an increase in slots.

DEPRIVATION

prived PCs cannot recover HP. If
prived for more than a day, they add
'atigue to inventory. Fatigue occupies
e slot and lasts until they can recover
safety. This effect is cumulative.

HEALING

noment's rest and a swig of water will
:ore lost HP, but may leave the party
nerable. **Ability** loss requires a week's
:t and the aid of a skilled healer.

SPELLBOOKS

:llbooks contain a single spell and take
one item slot. Anyone can cast a spell by
ding a Spellbook in *both hands* and
ding its contents aloud. Casting a spell
ls **Fatigue** to the PC's inventory.

:n time and safety, PCs can *enhance* a
ll without any additional cost. If they
deprived or in danger, a WIL save may
required to avoid terrible consequences.

ACTIONS

On their turn, a character may move up to
40ft and take up to one action. Actions may
include *casting a spell*, *attacking*, making a
second *move*, or other reasonable activities.
Actions, attacks, and movements take place
simultaneously. Whenever turn order is
uncertain, the PCs should make a DEX save
to see if they go before their enemies.

Retreating from a dangerous situation
always requires a successful DEX save, as
well as a safe destination to run to.

COMBAT

The attacker rolls their weapon die and
subtracts the target's Armor, then deals the
remaining total to their opponent's HP.

Before calculating damage to HP, subtract
the target's **Armor** value from the result of
damage rolls. Shields and similar armor
provide a bonus defense (e.g. +1 Armor),
but only while the item is held or worn.
No one can have more than 3 Armor.

Unarmed attacks always do 1d4 damage. If
multiple attackers target the same foe, roll
all damage dice and keep the single highest
result. If attacking with **two weapons** at
the same time, roll both damage dice and
keep the highest.

If an attack is **impaired**, the damage die is
reduced to 1d4, regardless of weapon. If the
attack is **enhanced**, the attacker rolls 1d12.
Attacks with the **blast** quality affect all area
targets, rolling separately for each.

DAMAGE

If an attack reduces a PC's HP exactly to 0,
refer to the **Scars** table (page **14**).

Damage that reduces a target's HP **below** 0
decreases their STR by the remainder. They
must then make a STR save to avoid **critical
damage.** Failure takes them out of combat,
dying if left untreated.

Having 0 STR means **death;** having 0 DEX
is paralysis; having 0 WIL is delirium.

Printed in Great Britain
by Amazon

36876264R00020

Whispers of a Weary Moon

Dreamer Poetry

Pale witness to whispered vows, the moon keeps secrets in these quiet boughs.

Preface

This book blooms from silence, an echo chamber whispering secrets of solitude. No desolate plains here, but jungles of self-discovery where shadows dance and moons confide. No pronouncements, just raw musings on the human heart, laid bare by aloneness.

These poems waltz with the universe, some aching with absence, others singing of self-sufficiency. In rustling leaves and murmuring waves, nature whispers solace. Turn the page, dear reader, and let the silence hold you. May these echoes not echo loneliness, but the vibrant chorus of your soul.

Contents

Footprints in the Fading Sand

Etched whispers on the shore, a fleeting dance,

Footprints in the sand, a losing trance.

The tide's cold breath devours each shallow rhyme,

Leaving echoes of a path, lost to time.

Sun-kissed impressions, shadows in the light,

A tale half-told, in morning's gentle bite.

Who carved these stories, whispered in the breeze?

Where did they wander, through rustling seas?

A lone gull circles, cries a mournful sound,

As waves erase the whispers, unbound.

Was it a child's laughter, skipping free?

Or lovers' footsteps, yearning by the sea?

Perhaps a nomad, with a wandering soul,

Or dreams adrift, escaping life's control.

The sand holds secrets, whispers to the shore,

But fleeting moments cannot linger more.

Yet in the fading lines, a beauty lives,

A poem written, where the ocean gives.

For even memories, washed away with tide,

Leave whispers in our hearts, where they reside.

So let us walk, and leave our marks behind,

Embrace the transient, know we cannot bind.

For like the footprints, etched in fleeting sand,

Life's moments pass, but leave us hand in hand.

Where Trees Converse in Rustling Tongues

Beneath a canopy of emerald lace,

Sunlight dribbles through in dancing grace.

Where mossy giants touch the whispering sky,

And secrets stir, on unseen branches lie.

In rustling tongues, the ancient cedars speak,

Of moonlit dances, secrets dark and meek.

The elms, they murmur legends lost in time,

Of whispered wishes, love's forgotten chime.

The birch, with silver fingers, taps a tune,

A mournful symphony beneath the moon.

And willows weep, their branches long and low,

For dreams forgotten, where no roses grow.

The oak, a patriarch, with gnarled and mighty hand,

Speaks tales of storms that swept across the land.

Of lives entwined, in roots that intertwine,

A tapestry of ages, whispered, line by line.

The wind, a messenger, on currents light,

Carries their voices through the fading light.

And I, who listen, with a heart unbound,

Find solace in the whispers, all around.

In rustling tongues, the forest breathes and sighs,

A symphony of secrets, reaching for the skies.

Where whispers weave a magic in the air,

And ancient wisdom lingers, everywhere.

So let me wander, in this leafy hush,

Where trees converse, and souls are gently brushed.

For in their language, whispered soft and low,

I find the peace, that only forests know.

Sunsets Painted for One

The sky ignites, a canvas vast and wide,

Where whispers of the sun in colors glide.

A symphony of orange, kissed with flame,

Burns down the day, whispers its dying name.

Crimson bleeds to gold, then melts to rose,

Each brushstroke etched in twilight's fading doze.

Clouds, like ships adrift in fiery seas,

Sail westward, chased by shadows on the breeze.

No shared eyes gaze upon this closing scene,

No hand in hand to claim this vibrant sheen.

A lonely heart watches the day descend,

Sunsets painted for one, with no pretend.

The hush descends, a velvet curtain spun,

Stars begin their dance, diamonds one by one.

A solitary sigh drifts on the air,

As twilight's gentle fingers touch the hair.

Yet, in this solitude, a beauty lies,

A whispered secret in the sunset's eyes.

For in the quietude, the soul takes flight,

And paints its own dreams on the canvas of the night.

So let the colors bleed, let shadows fall,

This sunset's mine, to cherish, to enthrall.

For even solo hearts find solace here,

Sunsets painted for one, precious and clear.

Cartography of Quietude

In hushed atlases, where moonlight maps the way,

I trace the rivers of silence, whispers soft astray.

Through valleys veiled in dusk, where secrets gently sleep,

My pen inks shadows, shadows secrets, secrets deep.

On starlit vellum, I chart the sighs of ancient trees,

Where wind-borne lullabies rustle mysteries.

A feather's fall, a moth's hushed wing, a spider's silver thread,

These etch the contours of stillness, where dreams lie softly
spread.

I chart the moonlit pools, where fireflies ignite,

A constellation mirrored, burning ever bright.

Through meadows hushed with dewdrops, where crickets chirp
and hum,

I map the path of peace, where worries find their tomb.

On canvas woven from starlight, I sketch the sleeping town,

Chimney smoke like wispy lines, secrets settling down.

Beneath the velvet cloak of night, where dreams begin to bloom,

The map unfolds, a tapestry woven in the moonlit room.

No compass guides, no ruler reigns, no city claims this land,

This cartography of quietude, held solely in my hand.

A map inscribed with starlight, where whispers find their voice,

A secret atlas, where the soul may quietly rejoice.

So hush, now, traveler, and let my map unfold,

The path to slumber's solace, a story yet untold.

In ink of stardust, a journey lies in wait,

To traverse the map of quietude, and seal the day's debate.

For in this cartography, where shadows softly meet,

The soul finds solace, and the heart, its tranquil beat.

Where Inner Landscapes Bloom

Behind the eyelids, worlds unfold,

Vast vistas painted, dreams untold.

A canvas woven from whispers deep,

Where shadows dance and secrets sleep.

Sun-dappled meadows bathed in blue,

Where fireflies on wishes flew.

Crystal rivers carved in thought,

Flowing through fears long fought.

Mountains sculpted from desire,

Reach for galaxies set afire.

Caves of memories, soft and dim,

Echo with lullabies within.

Ancient forests of resilience stand,

Rooted in faith, unmoved by sand.

Gentle breezes of forgiveness blow,

Whispering tales of letting go.

In this realm, the soul takes flight,

Unfettered by the fading light.

A symphony of colors hum,

Where every wish can overcome.

So close your eyes, and journey there,

To landscapes bloomed in silent prayer.

Where stardust whispers from the trees,

And inner wonders set you free.

Rendezvous with the Unknown Self

In the hush of dawn, where shadows cling,

I steal away, on the silent wing.

No map to guide, no path defined,

Just whispers faint upon the wind.

Through tangled woods, where sunlight sleeps,

Past slumbering ponds where moonlight weeps,

My footsteps falter, senses strain,

To glimpse the face I dare not name.

Within the cave of self-concealed,

Where fears and doubts lie unconcealed,

A mirror waits, its surface bare,

To show the truths I cannot bear.

But courage flares, a flickering flame,

I breathe it deep, and call my name.

The veil dissolves, the shadows bend,

And there I stand, at journey's end.

Eyes that hold a stranger's gaze,

A heart that echoes through the maze,

A soul etched fine, with scars and grace,

This is the self I meet face-to-face.

Tears fall like rain, then laughter rings,

As acceptance dawns on unseen wings.

No longer lost, no longer blind,

The unknown self becomes my kind.

In sunlit meadows, hand in hand,

We walk as one, across the land.

Embrace the darkness, welcome light,

Rendezvous with the unknown self, ignite.

The Compass Points Within

No needle spins, no north star gleams,

No parchment map unfolds its seams,

The journey lies within the soul,

Unfurling stories yet untold.

The compass points are whispered dreams,

Of sunlit glades and moonlit streams,

Of mountain peaks that pierce the sky,

And valleys nestled soft and shy.

Each beat of heart, a guiding drum,

To distant lands where shadows hum,

Where courage whispers in the breeze,

And doubt dissolves like fallen leaves.

The east wind calls with sunrise gold,

To forge new paths, be strong and bold,

The south wind sighs with ancient lore,

Of secrets whispered evermore.

The west wind paints a fiery hue,

On horizons stretching ever new,

And north wind sings of glacial call,

To face the depths and stand up tall.

No metal bound, no fixed decree,

The compass points reside in thee,

A whispering symphony unseen,

Guiding through darkness to the green.

So trust the map your spirit weaves,

Embark on quests where intuition cleaves,

For with each breath, each step you take,

The compass points within awake.

Rekindling the Inner Flame

Beneath the ash of days grown weary,

Where embers sleep and doubt holds sway,

A spark persists, a whisper fiery,

Promising a brighter, warmer way.

With gentle breath, I fan the embers,

Embrace the faintest wisp of glow,

Unravel layers of slumbering embers,

Where strength, once vibrant, used to flow.

Old fears may whisper, shadows linger,

But hope ignites, a steady hand,

Feeding kindling, memories that linger,

Of dreams untamed, a promised land.

Each tender crackle, a whispered story,

Of passion's dance, of laughter's song,

Of soaring spirit, once full of glory,

That yearns to rise, where it belongs.

I coax the flame, with trembling fingers,

Embrace the warmth, the flickering light,

Let go of burdens, doubt that lingers,

And step into the radiant night.

The inner fire, a phoenix rising,

Consumes the doubts, the ashes past,

With burning eyes, I'm now baptizing,

My soul anew, at long last.

So let the flame embrace the darkness,

Let it dance and roar and set me free,

For I am more than ash and starkness,

Rekindled, wild, eternally.

Haiku of a Lonely Star

In velvet cloak, a lone star gleams,

A teardrop lost in cosmic seas,

Yearning weaves through silent dreams,

Whispers waltz with galaxies.

No mirrored soul in stardust swirl,

Across the stage, the echoes sigh,

A lonely waltz, a moonlit curl,

Diamonds weep while shadows fly.

Ages etched in solo grace,

On stardust skin, a frozen tear,

A million waltzes paint the space,

But solitude clings, ever near.

The moon, a watcher, pale and still,

Reflects a symphony of light,

Where constellations dance at will,

Love's embers in the endless night.

Hope, a comet's fleeting spark,

Across the canvas, vast and black,

A whispered song, a celestial arc,

A silent yearning on the track.

In this grand symphony of stars,

Each note, though born in lonely flight,

A universe unfolds, unbars,

A melody taking wing in light.

So shines the star, a beacon bold,

In the eternal, starry sea,

Dreaming tales yet to be told,

Of waltzes danced in ecstasy.

A whispered wish on stardust spun,

A melody for dawning's grace,

The lonely star finds its own sun,

Until a new waltz finds its place.

A Refuge for the Weary Heart

When shadows steal the sun's caress,

And burdens bend the spirit low,

A haven waits, a gentle dress,

To mend the wounds and help it grow.

Amidst the boughs, where whispers sigh,

In mossy hush, a sanctuary,

Where sunlight paints the dappled sky,

And leaves embrace in verdant symphony.

On verdant moss, the soul reclines,

Beneath the canopy's soft gaze,

The symphony of rustling vines

Hums lullabies in sunlit maze.

No echoes of the world intrude,

Just wind-kissed leaves and whispered prayer,

A tranquil peace, a solitude,

Where healing streams like morning air.

The heart, once fractured, finds its beat,

In nature's rhythm, calm and slow,

Where worries bloom and gently greet,

Then melt like dewdrops in the glow.

So wander in, where troubles cease,

And weary limbs on roots recline,

The refuge holds, a whispered peace,

A balm for hearts that yearn to shine.

For in the fold of earth and sky,

The weary soul finds solace sweet,

Where broken wings begin to fly,

And hearts find refuge, safe and complete.

The Long Song of Longing

In hushed heartbeats, yearning takes its flight,
A feathered whisper through the starlit night.
Across the plains where shadows gently creep,
The long song of longing hums, in slumber deep.

For distant shores where moonlit oceans gleam,
For faces faded, lost in a vanished dream.
For voices stilled, in echoes soft and low,
The embers glow, refusing to let go.

Through sun-drenched meadows, where the wildflowers sway,
And whispered secrets dance on lips of day,
A tender ache, a yearning undefined,
For solace sought, in whispers on the wind.

Through city canyons, where steel giants rise,
A lonely echo in a million eyes.
For touch ungrasped, for words unspoken clear,
The long song lingers, tinged with a silent tear.

But in the hush, where twilight paints the sky,

A glimmer dawns, a solace lullaby.

In memories held, in threads of time so fine,

The longing weaves, a tapestry divine.

For love still blooms, in whispers faint and true,

And hope ascends, in skies of morning dew.

The long song lingers, a bittersweet refrain,

A promise whispered, that love won't fade in vain.

So let it rise, on wings of silver night,

The long song of longing, bathed in moonlit light.

For in its depths, a truth we all confess,

The yearning heart, forever finds its bliss.

Embracing the Empty Chair

The chair sits vacant, sun-kissed dust,
A vacant throne, where laughter thrust.
No touch of form, no whispered name,
But whispers linger, fanning flame.

I touch the cool, where sunlight lies,
Seek solace in the memory's disguise.
Ghostly fingers leave their trace,
A phantom warmth in this cold space.

But grief, like rain, can nourish still,
Where broken roots find fertile will.
The chair, a chalice, love's pure hold,
Embraces absence, stories told.

So I lean in, whisper to the hush,
Embrace the space, a gentle crush.
For in this void, love brightly beams,
A steady ember, in whispered dreams.

The sun will set, the stars ignite,

And on this chair, love takes its flight.

Embraced in darkness, hand in hand,

We'll dance forever, on memory's sand.

The moon will wane, the dawn anew,

The empty chair, reborn, brand new.

A vessel filled with memories sweet,

A love eternal, bittersweet.

And though the void may linger still,

This chair whispers, against the chill.

Of laughter shared, and love's embrace,

A phantom comfort, in this lonely space.

So let me hold, and let me grieve,

In this still place, where memories weave.

The empty chair, a gentle guide,

To where your love will always reside.

Printed in Great Britain
by Amazon